W9-CEK-601

My Feet Are Webbed and Orange

by Joyce Markovics

Consultant:
Christopher Kuhar, PhD
Executive Director
Cleveland Metroparks Zoo
Cleveland, Ohio

BEARPORT
PUBLISHING

New York, New York

Credits
Cover, © Wolfgang Kruck/Shutterstock; 4–5, © Attila JANDI/Shutterstock;
6–7, © Michiel Vaartjes/Minden Pictures; 8–9, © Susan Montgomery/Shutterstock;
10–11, © Matyas Arvai/Shutterstock; 12–13, © Michael Ransburg/Shutterstock;
14–15, © Nature Picture Library/Alamy Stock Photo; 16–17, © Jerry Monkman/
Nature Picture Library; 18–19, © Tim Plowden/Alamy Stock Photo; 20–21, © Tim
Plowden/Alamy Stock Photo; 22, © pchoui/iStock; 23, © Eric Isselee/Shutterstock;
24, © Eric Isselee/Shutterstock.

Publisher: Kenn Goin
Senior Editor: Joyce Tavolacci
Creative Director: Spencer Brinker
Design: Debrah Kaiser

E
598.33
MAR

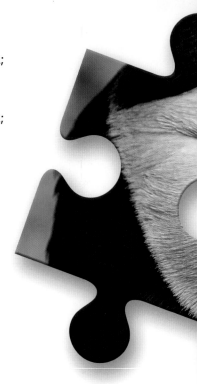

Library of Congress Cataloging-in-Publication Data

Names: Markovics, Joyce L., author.
Title: My feet are webbed and orange / by Joyce Markovics.
Description: New York, New York : Bearport Publishing, [2017] | Series: Zoo
  clues 2 | Audience: Ages 6–9._ | Includes bibliographical references and
  index.
Identifiers: LCCN 2016006801 | ISBN 9781944102623 (library binding)
Subjects: LCSH: Atlantic puffin–Juvenile literature. | Puffins–Juvenile
  literature. | Zoo animals–Juvenile literature.
Classification: LCC QL696.C42 M3585 2017 | DDC 598.3/3–dc23
LC record available at http://lccn.loc.gov/2016006801

For more information, write to Bearport Publishing Company, Inc., 45 West 21st Street, Suite 3B,
New York, New York 10010. Printed in the United States of America.

10 9 8 7 6 5 4 3 2 1

Contents

What Am I?

Look at my beak.

4

It is large and
colorful.

5

I have two wings.

6

They are long and grayish black.

7

My chest and
belly are soft
and white.

I have small,
round eyes.

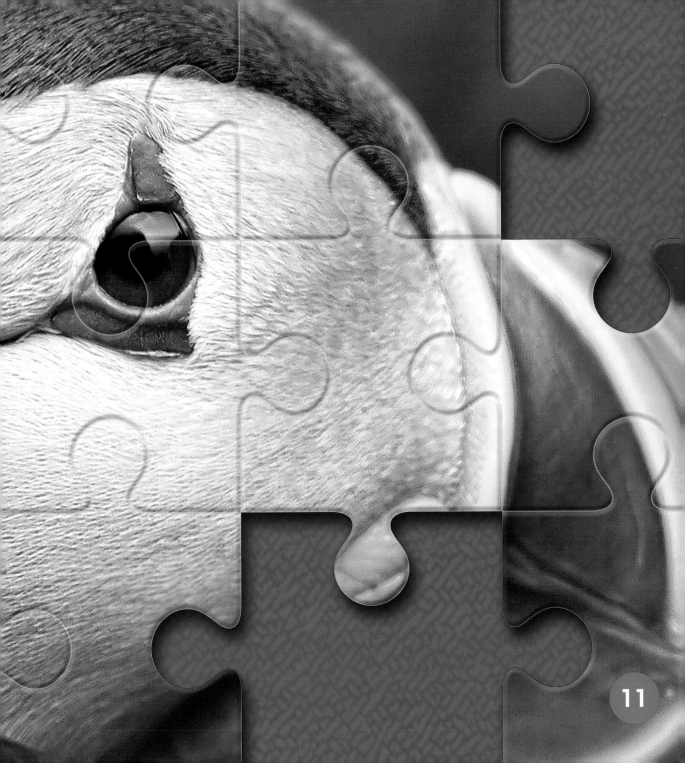

My tail feathers
are short
and black.

12

I have a small,
stocky body.

My feet are
webbed
and orange.

17

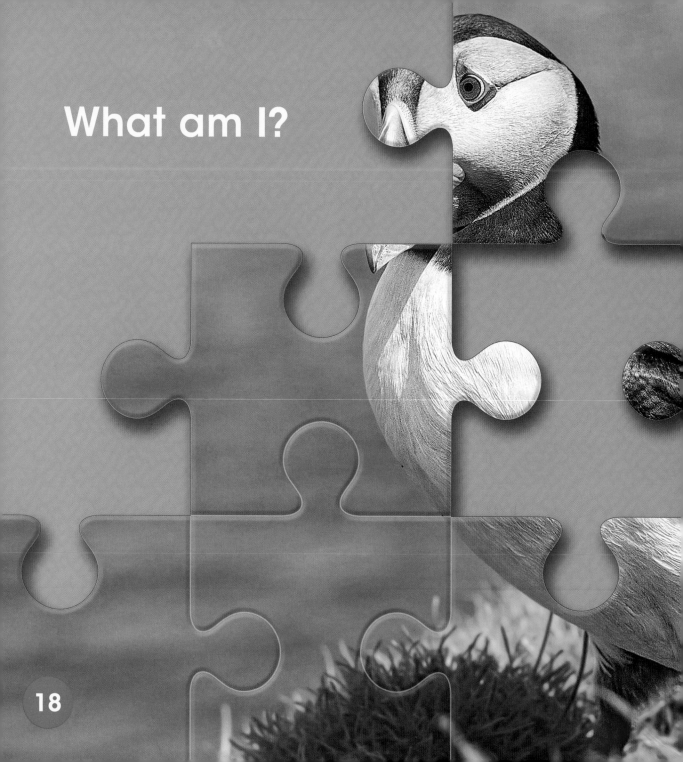

What am I?

Let's find out!

I am an
Atlantic puffin!

21

Animal Facts

Atlantic puffins are birds that spend most of their lives at sea. Puffins are great fliers. They can also dive deep underwater, using their wings as paddles.

More Atlantic Puffin Facts

Food:	Small fish
Size:	About 10 inches (25 cm) tall
Weight:	About 17.5 ounces (496 g)
Life Span:	20 years or more
Cool Fact:	A puffin can flap its wings 400 times per minute and fly up to 55 miles per hour (88.5 kph)!

Adult Atlantic Puffin Size

Where Do I Live?

Atlantic puffins live on and near seacoasts in the North Atlantic Ocean.

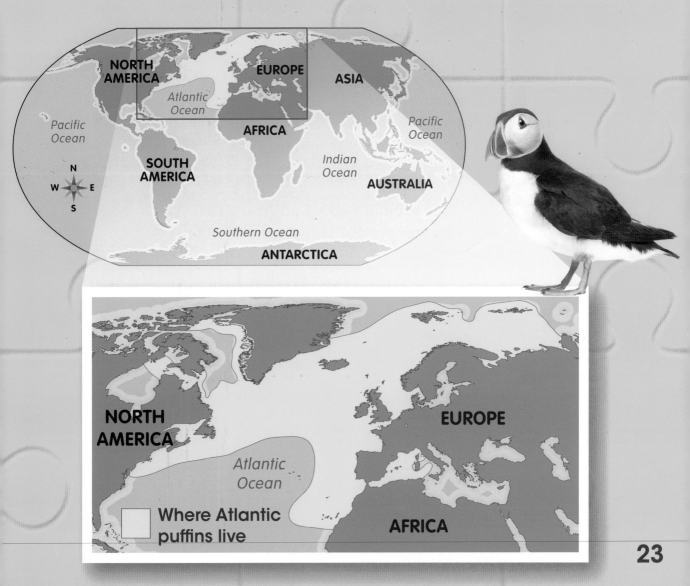

Where Atlantic puffins live

Index

Read More

Gibbons, Gail. *The Puffins Are Back!* New York: HarperCollins (1991).

Squire, Ann O. *Puffins (True Books: Animals).* New York: Scholastic (2007).

Learn More Online

To learn more about puffins, visit **www.bearportpublishing.com/ZooClues**

About the Author

Joyce Markovics lives in a very old house in Ossining, New York. She enjoys spending time with furry, finned, and feathered creatures.